Diapers and Dominoes (D.A.D.)

The Father's Blueprint For Raising AMAZING Kids

(hint: 'we need lots of help')

H. Darnell Cail

ISBN: 979-8-9944596-1-4 (Paperback)
ISBN: 979-8-9944596-0-7 (eBook)

Book Cover & typesetting assistance by manuscript2ebook.com

Table of Contents

Introduction

The Fatherhood Revolution: Starting Strong and Enlisting Others

Welcome brothers, to "Diapers And Dominoes"(D.A.D.). This ain't just some book I put together; it's a piece of my soul, written for guys like us who are out there in the trenches of this crazy life. It's short, it's sweet, and it cuts out all that junk and stupid stuff. What I set out to do with this book is way bigger than just helping you throw a party; it's about igniting a whole new movement, a "revolution of recommitted fathers," equipping us for the incredible, lifelong journey of being truly great dads. While I offer up a fresh alternative to traditional baby showers for the dad-to-be and his crew, my deep-down purpose goes way beyond just one evening: it's all about dishing out encouraging guidance on how to be a top-tier father throughout your child's whole life. I truly believe this is essential and must-have information for every man and father, and for the mothers who wish to understand and empower the fathers in their lives. If you want to get straight to that part of the book, go to chapter 4 now. But stop by chapter 2 first to read "Real Guy-Code". Otherwise, let's keep going...

A New Vision for Fatherhood: Empowerment and Unity

Deservingly so, the spotlight shines on the expecting mom during pregnancy and the early parenting days, often leaving us expecting dads feeling a little awkward or pushed to the side at traditional baby showers. For those who do not know... here's a News Flash!: the father is just as excited and hyped-up as the mother about their soon-to-be-born child, but we just wanna express that excitement in our own way. As guys, we get it! A lot of attention is rightfully showered on the mother as she carries that "precious cargo," but the expectation for a man to put on fake smiles and linger around the house, killing time is simply not cool. Diapers and Dominoes directly tackles this by offering a men-only alternative: a space where dads can celebrate without all the pretense, a good ol' guys-night-out setting that eliminates these issues permanently. It's not just a party; it's like the first wave of this amazing journey of fatherhood, designed to revitalize the dad-to-be and give him a boost of excitement. This book, my gift to you, empowers men to fully embrace their vital role, while unifying us in the shared and noble cause of raising great children.

Chapter 1

The Privilege, The Responsibility, The Journey

I've come to realize, in my old age, that being a dad isn't a *Right*; it's a gift and a privilege, so please cherish it. This journey, I promise you, is some hard work. If you ever catch yourself thinking it's easy, that's your cue to "check yourself" because you might be missing something crucial. From the moment of conception, through infancy, childhood, adolescence, and into their young adult years, our role is constantly shifting and growing. We are a huge influence in our children's lives, and everything we say and do; Everything we don't say and don't do...it all matters to our kids. I'll openly admit right here that I am no expert in parenting...far from it as a matter of fact, but my aim is to share many lessons learned, ah-hah's, do's and don'ts and simple 'hindsight' that God has blessed me with re-membering.

The Power of Brotherhood: Why Men Need Each Other for the Greater Cause

My own walk-through life and what I've seen with my own eyes has laid bare a profound truth that I hold dear: _men need to support, encourage and reprimand each other_. Sadly, I've seen fathers who aren't doing right by their children or their significant other. They were in desperate need of having a true male crew that would get them on track and hold him accountable. Experience has shown me that women, "wonderful" as they are, often struggle to motivate a father to step up, or go back home or take care of his kid. This is where our male circle becomes absolutely indispensable, truly unifying fathers in a common purpose. The Diapers and Dominoes (DAD) concept, and this book as a whole, is built on my fervent hope that it will serve as an opportunity to remind dads and dads-to-be of four crucial things: (1) How blessed we are to have a chance to shape a life (2) How huge the responsibility is (3) How important it is to have a strong support group and (4) How much fun you can have now and during the years raising a child. These events, in my vision, are designed to be more than just a single night of fun; they are meant to be a _"recurring revolution of recommitted fathers for years to come"_. This support network, I believe with all my heart, is vital. As you read, you'll see how this brotherhood can provide the necessary encouragement and accountability throughout your parenting journey, urging you, as I've been urged, to ask for help and support from other fathers when facing challenges. This unity empowers us all for the greater cause of raising exceptional children.

Understanding and Supporting the Mother's Journey: A Unified Front

While this book focuses on the father's experience, it is critical, and something I've personally learned, to acknowledge and understand the mother's journey as well. We will spend months of dealing with a pregnant woman: walking on eggshells (trying not to say the wrong thing), cleaning up, being more sensitive, being sex deprived, being considerate, lying about how...I mean telling her how pretty she is pregnant and worst of all...LISTENING. This period, culminating in the Diapers and Dominoes event, offers a moment for the dad-to-be to be revitalized before the new delivery. Beyond the pregnancy, I think that our primary focus during the first two years of our child's life must include being mentally prepared to support the mother as she recovers and tries to regain some normalcy in her life. This ain't a "favor" we're doing; helping the mother equates to helping the child. It's about recognizing her struggle, sharing the load, and ensuring her well-being, which directly impacts the child's environment. This book, I hope, provides insights that inspire mothers by demonstrating a father's deep commitment to a unified parenting front, fostering collaboration and mutual respect.

Adapting to Your Child's Evolving Needs: A Lifelong Commitment Fatherhood

Our role as dads isn't a static role we can just set and forget; it requires constant adjustment of our parental style and focus as the child enters new stages of their life. The later chapters of this book, kicking off at Chapter 4, offer specific guidance and advice that I've gathered from other fathers and my own first-hand lessons as a dad, spanning from their first 2 years all the way to 25 years old. Each age bracket, I've seen, brings its own unique challenges and rewards, calling for a flexible and attentive approach. You'll learn, as I have, to be a dad first, then a friend, recognizing that your primary role is to teach, encourage, mold, provide and discipline.

Chapter 2

Real 'Guy-Code': Principles for the Dedicated Dad

My brothers, this chapter lays out a foundational set of principles, what I call "Real 'Guy Code'," for every father to truly embrace. It's not just some list of individual rules; it's a shared blueprint for fatherhood that should be memorized and proudly posted on your frig. More importantly, it is intended to serve as a common understanding for the brotherhood of fathers, providing a framework for mutual support, encouragement, and even that gentle reprimand when one of us needs to get right. When we gather with other dads, these rules can be the basis for our discussions, shared challenges, and collective accountability, unifying us for the greatest cause: raising a great kid.

A Shared Blueprint for Fatherhood: Our Collective Vows

As I laid out in the introduction, I truly believe men need to support, encourage and reprimand each other. By understanding and committing to this code collectively, I know we strengthen the foundation of our fatherhood journey and the support network around us, empowering each man to strive for excellence and uniting us in our shared responsibilities.

The Top 20 Rules for Successful Fathers

1. First, you must realize that you don't deserve to be a dad...it's a gift and a privilege; cherish it

2. It's hard work when you are being a great dad...if you ever get the sense it's easy, check yourself; you could be missing something

3. If you don't think that your kid(s) is/are better than every other kid in the world, then you SUCK as a dad

4. You are a huge influence in your child's life. Everything you say and do; Everything you don't say and don't do...it all matters to your kid

5. Time with you is precious to your child. Give them your undivided attention

6. Be a person who your kids can be proud of...note: this has nothing to do with what you do for a living or how much money you make

7. Don't be abusive to them, their mother or anyone around them...it will have a damaging effect on them short-term and long-term

8. Show genuine interest in what they do. If you don't understand it or like it, simply ask them to explain it and tell you why they like it

9. 'Show' your kids that you are a hard worker

10. Be a God-fearing man, pray around your child and as often as possible, take your child to church with you

11. Support your kids no matter what...socially, financially and emotionally

12. Don't allow a strained relationship with their mother deter you from loving and supporting your child. If you do, the child loses...twice

13. Be involved in their life; don't miss out...you WILL regret it later

14. Be a dad first...then a friend. You are there to teach, encourage, mold, provide and discipline

15. Always be honest with them...lying and sugar-coating will cripple them and diminish the trust and respect they have for you.

16. Be fun to be around...don't be so hard and scary

17. Don't give them everything they want...instead, give them access to everything and teach them how to obtain it

18. Demonstrate your respect for the child's mother and respect others while the child is in your presence

19. Be tough on your son, but fair...he can take it
20. Last, but not least...your family is your first priority; everything else can wait...especially the job.

These rules are the backbone of a successful father's life. They are a constant reminder of the dedication required throughout this parenting journey.

CHAPTER 3

The Kick-Off Celebration

This chapter details the Guys-Only baby showers, affectionately referred to as "**D**iapers **A**nd **D**ominoes" (D.A.D.). It is far more than just a guys-night-out event; it's like the official inaugural gathering of the fatherhood brotherhood. This informal, yet structured, plan serves as the founding ritual for a unified group of men dedicated to being great dads.

At traditional baby showers, I've often seen the dad-to-be looking awkward, isolated, and meandering around the house killing time...maybe cooking or drinking or watching TV. It most cases, it just doesn't seem like he's having a good time. He is merely doing whatever he needs to do to stay out of the way, as the mother-to-be gets the attention. Diapers and Dominoes will eliminate this issue...permanently. This men-only alternative is specifically cooked up to let us express our excitement in our own way. It's a unique chance for men to come together to solidify a crucial support group for the dad-to-be. This event is a critical moment for us all to be reminded of how important it is to have a strong support group as we embark on the monumental task of shaping a life. It empowers us to take on our role with confidence and unites us in a shared journey.

There are several options for an epic **Guys Night theme** to celebrate a new arrival.

1. Diapers and Dominoes
2. Pampers and Poker
3. Luvs and Laughs
4. Huggies and Happy Hour

The "Diapers and Dominoes" theme is the one that started it all for me and the fellas...and has become the widely acceptable phrase to refer to any guys-only baby shower. As you might have guessed, the last term/phrase of each of the options tells you the main activity or setting for the celebration. It's either a domino night, a poker night, a comedy night or a happy hour. I will not go into too much detail now, but I will provide a high-level overview of how the celebration will go.

Diapers and Dominoes or Pampers and Poker can be done at someone's house, apartment, backyard or clubhouse. This is informal fun but it still requires some level of planning. All details of everything you would need are provided in the Appendix of this book. Luvs and Laughs....

you guessed it, this is simply a planned night at a comedy show. Because of this, someone will need to be proactive by searching for the right comedian/right night to attend the show. They would need to coordinate the attendees so everyone could secure tickets in advance. Finally, Huggies and Happy Hour has always been one of the best options. This is because the staff and strangers alike love to help you celebrate. The key here is location, location, location. This could be a sports bar, a restaurant, a wine bar, etc. Organizing this with the venue's management is the vital task, to make it a memorable evening.

Skip to the Appendix to begin planning for either of the 4 options.

Otherwise, Let's talk about how you will grow into an incredible dad

Chapter 4

The Fatherhood Journey Begins (The First 2 Years)

Nurturing Your Child, Supporting Your Partner

The celebrations are all over, the baby is here, the in-laws have gone home and now Reality has a cruel way of kicking you in the balls each day....you should be asking yourself, "Now what?". This chapter marks the beginning of your journey to "Being a Great Dad Through the Years" ... focusing on the crucial first two years of your child's life. This stage demands significant adjustment of your parental style and focus, a deep understanding of the mother's needs, and an unwavering commitment to your child's well-being. It is a period where Dads need to ask for help and support from other fathers and their broader community. This brotherhood provides crucial unity and empowerment during this intense, formative period, ensuring no father feels alone in the early challenges.

The Dawn of Reality: Adjusting to New Life. During these first two years, my primary focus is crystal clear: to ensure that the baby is in a safe environment, where he/she can feel love and is provided for. Gents, this is NOT a passive role; it demands active participation and, for many, some serious lifestyle adjustments. Personally, my initial thought of having "more free time" was WRONG!!! I had to cut my hanging-out time almost totally out for the first 6 months and adjust my work schedule to ensure that I had consistent hours. This might take you out of your comfort zone, but it will prove beneficial in the long run. This foundational period, I've learned, sets the pace for the entire parenting journey, emphasizing that it's hard work when you are being a great dad.

Understanding the Mother's Recovery and Needs: Our Unified Support. A critical aspect of being a great dad in these early years is recognizing that you also need to be mentally prepared and positioned to support the mother as she recovers and tries to regain some normalcy in her life. This understanding is paramount because helping the mother equates to helping the child, plain and simple. This message, I believe, is vital for mothers to feel inspired by a father's empathetic approach to family well-being.

- **Equal Concern:** Admirably, most women I know plan on going back to work as soon as they have fully recovered and they feel comfortable with how the baby will be cared for in their absence. As the father, you should be equally concerned about the child's environment and play a primary role in making sure that happens.

- **Observant and Proactive:** I strive to be observant. I look around to see what needs to be done and simply Do It. I don't wait to be asked and I don't make the mother feel like I am "doing her a favor" by helping with MY own kid. This proactive approach is a cornerstone of supportive co-parenting.

- **Addressing Your Own "Baggage":** It's naïve to think fathers are perfect. Some of us have baggage and/or personalities that could be distracting (to put it mildly). Dad....Just KNOW that you have issues that you need to admit to and ADDRESS them. Don't deceive yourself into thinking fatherhood will make you a better man; it will take a lot of work and a lot of time and focus. The journey of raising your child often mirrors the journey of raising yourself. You are expected to adjust your life to provide for the child and correct any issues that could be detrimental to them, the mother and/or those who are caring for the child. This is where other fathers in your support group can provide honest feedback and accountability, unifying us in a commitment to personal growth for the sake of our families.

Your Indispensable Role: Equality in Caregiving. The traditional model where *"the man was always working and the mother was at home with the baby"* during that initial 6 months no longer applies. Having a job is no longer an excuse for men not to be home caring for his newborn. You are EQUALLY responsible for feeding the child, taking them to doctors' appointments, playing with them and nursing them through illness. This is about shared responsibility and deep involvement, demonstrating a unified parental front.

Creating a Secure and Nurturing Environment. Babies are incredibly perceptive. Babies can sense nurturing and affection; they can also sense anger, worry and frustration. My role, and yours, is to provide stability and love.

When You're Doing It Right, You Will...

- *Know Their Conditions:* Whether you live with the mother or not, it is your obligation to know and understand the living conditions the child is in. If there are any concerns, address them quickly; that is your responsibility.

- *Create Predictable Routines:* Babies thrive on routine because it gives them a sense of security. Establishing consistent patterns for feeding, napping, and bedtime helps both you and the baby.

- *Embrace Skin-to-Skin Contact*: Research has shown that holding your baby close improves bonding and regulates their heartbeat and body temperature. Dads, don't miss out—ditch the shirt and snuggle up.

- *Be a Master of the Soothing Arts*: I learned my baby's preferred calming methods. Dr. Harvey Karp's "5 S's" (swaddle, side/stomach, shush, swing, suck) are a lifesaver. When your baby cries, please test these methods—find the one that works and stick with it. Responding to your baby's cries, holding them, and being consistent helps them feel securely attached to you. So, when your baby cries at 3 a.m., don't just stare at the ceiling and hope your partner gets up—be the hero. This demonstrates active involvement and support for both child and mother.

- *Team Parenting*: I take the night shift occasionally. A well-rested mom is a happy mom, which translates to a happy household. This is a direct act of understanding the mother's struggle and actively supporting her.

***Reality Check:** Your house will never be fully clean, and there will be days when you're running on caffeine and hope. But those baby giggles and first milestones? Totally worth it, I promise you.

How The Guys Can Help....

- *Sharing the Sleep Deprivation and Practical Strategies*: This is where the brotherhood truly shines. I reach out to other dads in my support group. I share my struggles with sleep, ask for advice on soothing techniques, and discuss how I cut my hanging-out time (they'll already know that 😊). We don't just commiserate; we exchange practical hacks for managing the chaos, like creative ways to get a fussy baby to sleep. Knowing you're not the only one facing these challenges is a unifying and empowering feeling.

- *Collective Strategies for Supporting the Mother*: I often discuss with the fellas, how to best support our partners' recovery and transition back to normalcy. Other fathers, especially those whose partners have returned to work, can offer tested strategies for dividing household duties, creating space for mom to rest, or planning those much-needed date nights. This collective wisdom ensures a unified and effective approach to family well-being, directly contributing to the mother's ability to do her job without distractions.

- *Accountability for Personal Growth:* If I'm struggling with my own "baggage" or adjusting my lifestyle, my brotherhood can be a powerful force for accountability. They provide honest feedback and encouragement, reminding me that I am expected to adjust my life to provide for the child and to correct issues detrimental to the child, the mother and/ or those who are caring for the child. This mutual support empowers each man to confront his own challenges and be a better father, strengthening the entire male circle.

- _Observation, Learning, and Practical Relief:_ Parenting is more of an art, as opposed to a science or instruction book, so learning from others' experiences is invaluable. Try to be observant of how other parents, especially other dads, handle things and learn from both successes and challenges. More than just observation, please offer or accept practical help. A brother might offer to watch your baby for an hour so you can grab a quick nap or workout. This kind of hands-on support is invaluable and strengthens the bonds of our brotherhood.

***Time for Yourself and Your Partner:** Amidst all the demands, I always remember to find some time to relax, workout and treat the mom out to a date night from time to time. A well-rested and happy mom contributes to a happy household, and these moments help you stay grounded.

Child-Proofing Your Love: Safety First. As your baby starts to _explore_, safety becomes paramount. Please child-proof the house for a crawling/walking baby. Keep floors free of trash/debris and keep cabinets locked. Establish play areas and safe enclosures. This proactive step demonstrates your commitment to providing a safe environment.

I urge you to embrace the joy of these early years: Have fun getting to know your child, be observant, watching them crawl for the first time and hearing the first words. This stage is about **starting strong**, laying a foundation of love, security, and mutual support within your family and your crew of fellas, uniting and empowering you for the most important job in the world.

CHAPTER 5

Guiding The Explorer: (2-to-5 years old)

Teaching, Playing, and Setting Boundaries

As your child transitions from infancy, they enter a phase of intense exploration and learning. This is the season where everything changes—again. Your child is talking, walking, and running now. In one word, your child is **BUSY**, and that usually begins around the age of two. They explore everything. They push limits. They test patience. Daily.

This stage demands a shift in how you show up as a father. The focus moves from primary care to active teaching, guidance, and boundary setting. You are no longer just protecting a fragile infant—you are shaping a curious, determined little human who is actively trying to understand the world. This is also where the brotherhood of fatherhood matters most. Sharing insights, stories, and survival tactics with other dads becomes invaluable. Through shared experience, fathers are unified, empowered, and reminded that none of us are figuring this out alone.

One of the most significant changes during this stage is communication. Your child can now communicate, and that unlocks powerful new parenting opportunities. Your responsibility to assess their well-being and environment remains, but now you can talk with them. And once you can communicate with them, you can teach them. That single shift changes everything.

Reading becomes one of your most powerful tools. When you read to your child, you instantly become a "genius" in their eyes simply because you can read. Add emotion, voices, and enthusiasm to the stories, and you'll see their engagement increase. This is how curiosity is sparked. This is how a love for learning begins. Reading also becomes one of the simplest and most effective ways to bond while stimulating their growing mind.

Early education is not something to leave entirely to the mother, daycare, or preschool. Teaching your child words, numbers, and simple math is part of your role. Get involved. Don't sit on the bench as a spectator. Your active participation reinforces your place as a teacher and mentor, not just a helper.

There is an important mindset shift fathers must make during this stage. When you are caring for your own child, it is not called *babysitting*—it is parenting. Referring to it any other way will get you corrected quickly, believe me...I know 😊. Embrace your full responsibility without hesitation or disclaimers.

This stage also requires self-reflection. If you have unresolved issues, unhealthy habits, or behaviors that could negatively affect your child, the mother, or caregivers, you are expected to adjust. Your child is watching more than you realize. Self-awareness and self-improvement are no longer optional—they are part of the job description.

Taking your child out into the world is essential for their development. Family outings matter. If you are in a relationship, take your child with you when you leave the house. You will probably enjoy it—but if you don't, act like you do for your child's sake. Those shared experiences help your child feel safe, included, and connected. Public outings demand vigilance. You must keep your eyes on your child at all times—every second. Whether or not you believe in leashes or other tools, the rule is simple: always know where your child is. Many tragic stories begin with a momentary lapse in judgment. This is not an area for shortcuts.

You should also understand a hard truth early: your child will not behave better in public than they do at home. Learn who they are in familiar environments. Pay attention to what triggers frustration, how they respond to boundaries, and where challenges arise. Address these issues at home, because unresolved behavior only intensifies in public. Avoid becoming either the seemingly neglectful parent or the overly aggressive one. Consistency at home sets expectations everywhere else. These early years are foundational for teaching social concepts. This is when you introduce sharing and teach what the word "no" means. These lessons are not about control—they are about safety, respect, and preparing your child to interact with others. Placing your child around peers of similar ages, whether through daycare or playgroups, supports healthy social development.

As your toddler becomes more mobile and curious, safety remains a top priority. Secure your home. Remove harmful chemicals and dangerous objects from reach. At the same time, prepare yourself for the flood of questions. Your child will ask many—often random and repetitive. Answer when you can. When you can't, respond thoughtfully. Avoid dismissiveness. Your child is learning that you are a source of knowledge, patience, and reassurance. Clear communication with the mother becomes especially important during this stage. She should understand your schedule so planning can happen smoothly. You may be the parent with more flexibility for pickups, feedings, or childcare transitions. This cooperation shows unity and support.

If you and the mother are not together, consistency matters even more. Establish regular, predictable time with your child. When it's your turn, do not hand off your responsibilities to others. Nothing replaces your presence. Stability and reliability matter more than convenience. This stage is also when you begin to establish your identity in your child's mind. Introduce them to art, music, sports, and new experiences. Show them the world and let them gravitate toward what interests them. Do not force passions that aren't there. If you buy eight footballs and your child hasn't touched a single one, take the hint. This is the age when your child begins to understand who you are and why you matter. Spend this time wisely.

When you are doing it right, you begin to understand the **power of play**. Play fuels emotional growth and cognitive development. Hide-and-seek, blocks, dancing in the living room—these moments are shaping your child's brain in ways no worksheet ever could. Toddlers are language sponges. Narrate your actions. Ask questions. Expand their vocabulary naturally. At the same time, set clear boundaries, knowing your child will test every rule. Redirect unsafe behavior toward safe alternatives instead of relying on constant rejection. Discipline works best when it is consistent and rooted in love. Use positive phrasing whenever possible to encourage cooperation. This is also the stage where reality hits hard. You will say things like, "Why is there peanut butter on the dog?" "We don't lick grocery carts." "Please don't flush your action figures." Your patience will be tested daily. But remember—your child's curiosity is how they learn about the world, and how they teach you flexibility.

This season of fatherhood is demanding, but it is also where the fatherhood brotherhood becomes invaluable. Sharing strategies, holding one another accountable, laughing through the endless "why" phase, and offering practical support makes the journey manageable. Supporting the mother through consistent co-parenting reinforces stability and trust, especially when parents are not together. This stage will give you endless moments of joy, confusion, exhaustion, and laughter. Being a good father is not a solo mission. It is a long journey—one made stronger, wiser, and more meaningful when walked alongside other men who understand exactly what it takes.

CHAPTER 6

Shaping Character
(6-to-9 years old)

Involvement, Responsibility, and Open Dialogue

By this time, your child knows exactly who you are. That can work in your favor—or against you. They have an impression of you. You have a reputation. It didn't happen overnight, and it wasn't built on grand speeches or big moments. It was formed quietly, day by day, through tone, consistency, reactions, and follow-through. Whether you realize it or not, your child has been taking notes. Your child's perception of you is shaped by what they experience directly and by what they hear or feel from others. That part can feel uncomfortable. But here's the truth that should settle you: you still control more than you think. Perception isn't about being perfect. It's about being consistent and real.

You're no longer just Dad in the background. You're a reference point. You're the example they compare other men to. That realization alone forces a shift in how you move. This season requires another adjustment in your parenting style and focus, pushing you toward intentional character building, steady involvement, and honest conversation. It's also the stage where pride has to take a back seat. No one navigates school, friendships, early independence, and social pressure without help. This is where dads need other dads. When men lean on one another—through conversations, prayer, and shared experience—we create a support system strong enough to raise children who know right from wrong and have the confidence to stand on it.

One of the most underrated tools you have is honesty. Let your child know you're human. Tell them you make mistakes. Tell them you're learning too. And tell them that no matter what, you're committed to getting better. That kind of openness builds trust in a way authority never could.

The fact of the matter is that you can control their perception. Let them know that you are human...tell them that you make mistakes but you Always try to be better and improve. Believe me, they don't think parents make mistakes and it surprises them when you do. This reminds me of a funny personal story that humbles me every time I think of it. I ponder on it whenever I start to become arrogant and forget what's important. When my daughter was an infant, my son was almost 6 years old. He was our little helper and a great big brother. My son and I stayed home from school/work one day because we were sick with bad colds. I wanted to check to see if I had a fever, so I found the thermometer to take my temperature. As I put the thermometer in my mouth under my tongue...my son was next to me, staring at me, grimacing and frowning. With the thermometer in my mouth, I mumbled to him, "What's wrong with you? Why are you looking at me like that?" Looking totally disgusted, he slowly said, "You put the baby's booty thermometer in your mouth...you nasty". I hurt myself laughing when he said that, as I'm sure he had witnessed his mom checking the baby's bottom temperature on numerous occasions. 20 years later he still remembers it because it was the first time he ever felt like he knew something that I didn't. Being a role model isn't about projecting perfection. It's about showing your kids something real to respect. Show them that you work hard. Show them that you take responsibility when things go wrong. Show them that growth doesn't stop when you become an adult. Your actions will always speak louder than your intentions.

This season may be the most important time for hands-on involvement. What you say matters. What you don't say matters. What you do—and what you avoid—lands emotionally, even when you think it doesn't. Children at this age are emotional record keepers. They may forget details, but they remember how you made them feel. Now is when you can begin talking to them like a young man or a young lady. Real conversations start to happen. You can explain things instead of just directing them. When you speak to them with respect, they rise to it. Maturity grows where respect is planted.

Show up where they are. Be present at the games, the recitals, the practices, and the performances. Even the small ones. Especially the small ones. Be their biggest fan. Let them look into the crowd and find your face. That presence sends a message no motivational speech ever could: *You matter, and I'm paying attention.* Let them see your world too. Tell them about your day. Introduce them to your friends. Explain what you do for a living and why you do it. Show them how money works, how time matters, and how effort turns into results. These everyday conversations quietly prepare them for adulthood.

This is also the right age to teach responsibility in real ways. Giving them chores and holding them accountable isn't about control—it's about confidence. Responsibility builds independence, pride, and self-respect. Pair that with structure. A predictable routine after school gives them stability. You can switch things up, but your priorities should never feel random or confusing. Kids thrive when they know what's coming. Consistency is everything. Your child should know when they'll see you and when they'll hear from you. When that certainty disappears, doubt takes its place. Over time, inconsistency doesn't just damage trust—it teaches the wrong lesson. Even when you're not physically present, make sure your child knows how to reach you. Teach them that you are accessible, dependable, and steady. That belief becomes an anchor.

As children grow, their exposure to media and social influence expands quickly. Faster than most parents expect. This is where intentional parenting matters. Control what they are exposed to socially and electronically. Don't allow unlimited access to devices. Set boundaries early and clearly so expectations are understood, not debated. This is also where the fatherhood brotherhood becomes critical. Digital parenting is unfamiliar territory for most of us...and it continues to change aggressively as I write this book. Share strategies. Share mistakes. Learn together.

When things are clicking, you'll see certain traits take shape. Responsibility grows through chores like feeding pets or cleaning their room. Emotional intelligence develops when you help them identify what they're feeling—frustration, disappointment, excitement. This is a golden age for teaching empathy. Encourage exploration. Let them try sports, art, music, and hobbies without pressure. That's how grit forms—through curiosity, effort, and resilience. And then there are the questions. Endless questions. Deep ones. Random ones. "Why is the sky blue?" "Why do we pay taxes?" "Why can't we eat candy for dinner?" You'll learn quickly that saying, "That's a great question—let's look it up," is not a cop-out. It's leadership. It shows them how to think, not just what to think.

Through all of it, keep showing up. Keep being their biggest fan. Whether it's a championship game or a backyard magic show, your presence tells them they're worth your time. This is where the fatherhood brotherhood shows its value. Sharing mistakes keeps things honest. Talking about involvement keeps dads engaged. Supporting consistency—especially in co-parenting situations—creates stability where it's needed most. When fathers support one another, children feel it. Mothers feel it. Families benefit from it. This stage will challenge you. It will humble you. It will stretch your patience. It will also give you moments of joy you didn't see coming. Your child's curiosity will test you—and shape you. This is the season where your reputation is cemented. Not as a perfect father, but as a present one. And presence, when sustained over time, becomes legacy.

CHAPTER 7

Navigating Puberty's Waters (10-to-13 years old)

Trust, Communication, and Identity

The pre-teen years, my friend, bring with them turbulent waters. I will be short and sweet for this age period...One word: "Puberty!" so try your best to be patient. I do not know you, but I'm sure that this stage will require a significant adjustment to your parental style and focus; you are forced to move towards becoming an anchor of stability, a trusted confidant, and a guide through complex emotional and physical changes. It's a time when Dads need to ask for help and support from other fathers to navigate the unique challenges of tween development, especially regarding social media, identity, and sexuality, unifying us in sensitive guidance and protective care, and empowering us to build unwavering trust with our children.

Becoming "Uncool": Maintaining Stability and Trust

As my child enters their tween years, their perspective of me will inevitably shift. As a parent, you are gradually becoming an idiot to them, less smart and less cool. While this can be disheartening, your role becomes even more critical.

- Stability and Boundaries: Providing stability and setting clear boundaries should be your focus. (hint: your presence gives them a secure base amidst their internal and external changes)

- Trust and Openness: I strive to present myself as someone that they can trust and talk to...it becomes much more difficult to establish that after this period. This is a window of opportunity to solidify deep trust.

- Staying Connected to Their World: I keep my finger on the pulse of their lives; I am keenly aware of what they are exposed to and who their friends are. This will give you a good idea of who your child is.

- Discussing Social Challenges: This is a good time-period, to let them know the challenges of friendships, bullying and self-esteem. I teach them the concept of "You are defined by your friends" and give them "examples of healthy friendships and characteristics of 'good people'".

- <u>Avoid Being Preachy:</u> figure out a way of communicating with them that doesn't come across as preachy, overly critical or judgmental.

- <u>Ask Open-Ended Questions:</u> Instead of a simple "How was your day at school?", I try: "Tell me about your school day, starting with the thing that annoyed you most".

- <u>Practice Active Listening:</u> As they talk, practice 'active listening' (eye-contact, facial expressions and words like, "wow", "really?" or that's insane!). This shows genuine interest and makes them feel heard.

- <u>Teach Communication Skills:</u> Just as importantly, teach them what to do when speaking with someone (ex. make eye contact, sit up straight, speak clearly). These are vital life skills.

- <u>Relatable Lessons:</u> To teach a lesson or forewarn them, I sometimes tell a real story of someone I knew in school or look on the internet for related YouTube videos......and say to them, 'look at this crazy video'". Whatever works to keep their attention and the lines of communication open, do it.

- <u>Value Education:</u> I am involved in their schoolwork; I show them that it matters to me and their education is especially important. I encourage them to "try extremely hard to make good grades.

The Digital Dangers: Vigilance and Education

The digital world presents new and significant risks during these years and the teenage years.

- Social Media Caution: A personal "Word of Caution" highlights this danger for me: When my daughter was 12, she got that social media bug and was heavily involved with reading, posting and responding to other posts. At one point, this got out of hand and dangerous. It was discovered she was in a direct message chat with an older male "asking her to send 'sexy' pics of herself".

  - *Family Safety is your Number 1 Job*. My response was decisive... I changed how she engaged on social media, limited her access and educated her for the next several months on the do's and don'ts and dangers of social media. This experience underscores the need for constant vigilance and education. This is an area where fathers need to ask for help and support from other fathers who might know of online safety resources, therefore unifying us in safeguarding our children.

- Understanding Identity and Sexuality: I urge you to be VERY OBSERVANT between the ages of 12 and 14. You will notice subtle things about their personalities, their tendencies and mannerisms. Many parents have shared that during this period, their child had questions about their own sexuality... inquiring of *what's normal?* and/or *am I different?*

- <u>Unconditional Love for Sons</u>: Regarding our sons... Dads, please, please, please do not ostracize your son just because you 'feel' that he's not as masculine as you think you are or wish him to be. His sexuality choice has nothing to do with how strong he is mentally, physically or socially.

  - *Prioritize Safety and Health*: Please let him know often that you love him more than anything and that he can come to you about ANYTHING. It's your job to raise a flag and ask questions if you perceive anything "unhealthy or unsafe" going on in their life. This balanced approach combines love, trust, and protective parenting.

These are deeply personal and challenging conversations, where the wisdom and shared experiences from your support group of men, can be an invaluable resource for these sensitive areas.

When You're Doing It Right, You Will...

- <u>Teach Coping Skills</u>: This is not too early to teach tweens how to manage stress through techniques like "deep breathing or journaling". Being their emotional anchor during this rollercoaster phase is crucial.

- <u>Help Them Navigate Social Dynamics:</u> Friendships get tricky in these years. Teach them how to spot good friends and how to handle peer pressure. Role-playing scenarios (like saying "no" to something unsafe) can build their confidence.

- <u>Stay Engaged in Their World:</u> Even if Minecraft, Grow a Garden or TikTok isn't my thing, I show interest in their hobbies. I ask about their favorite YouTuber or join them for a gaming session. It's less about the activity and more about the connection.

- <u>Embrace Open Communication:</u> I talk to them about physical and emotional changes. I "normalize" topics like body image, friendships, and peer pressure. This open dialogue fosters trust and reduces shame.

- <u>Set Boundaries:</u> Screen time, curfews, and chores should have clear rules. Consistency is your best friend here.

- <u>Stay Involved:</u> They might roll their eyes when you ask about their day, but deep down, I know they appreciate it. Keep asking.

Supporting Mothers Through Shared Understanding and Unified Fronts: By actively engaging in these complex discussions, fathers gain a deeper understanding of the multifaceted challenges of the tween years. This enables us to provide more informed and empathetic support to mothers. Aligning on boundaries, social media rules, and responses to emotional outbursts allows both parents to present a unified front, which is crucial for the tween's stability and growth.

Listen to other dads, the guys, the crew, the fellas... can give their insights into how to maintain parental unity, preventing children from "splitting" parents.

A Humorous Look at Tweens: Tween logic is its own beast, I've discovered. They can be invincible one minute and the most misunderstood person on the planet the next. Brace yourself for phrases like: "You don't get it, Dad!" "Why are you so embarrassing?". Remember, it's the hormones talking. Keep your sense of humor and lean on your fatherhood brotherhood for shared stories and support during these often bewildering but vital years of identity formation.

The "teenage rollercoaster" is real, and I've ridden it. Engage other dads who can share effective coping mechanisms for dealing with mood swings, eye-rolls, and the feeling of being "uncool". Use humor to your advantage ("If you think I'm annoying now, just wait until I start texting you memes"). This can be a powerful bonding tool. Remind yourself not to take everything personally and to find the lighter side of parenting. This constant adjustment of your parental style and focus is key to building a resilient and trusting relationship with your child. Enlist, Enable and Empower other men to help you guide your child through this turbulent phase, reinforcing that collective strength makes the journey manageable.

CHAPTER 8

Partnership and Preparation (14-to-19 years old)

Guiding Your Teen Towards Adulthood

High school is a whole new animal and a beast of its own. For many, this period will mark a pivotal adjustment of their parental style and focus, transitioning from director to partner. The emphasis must be placed on preparing your teen for the independence of adulthood. This age frame is so challenging and near and dear to my heart, that I will speak in first person for most of this chapter. As I navigate these complex years, I remembered to ask for help and support from other fathers who have walked down this path.

High School: A New Frontier

To truly empathize with your teenager, I ask you to think back to who you were during this age span. Recall your thoughts, ideas, fears and struggles. When communicating, please limit the, "back in my day" or "when I was your age" lectures. Instead, I offer what I *would do* or *how I'd approach the situation* given the same circumstances they're faced with. More importantly, I tell them "Why" I would do those things. This empathetic and instructive approach fosters connection rather than defensiveness.

From Handholding to Partnership: Shifting Parental Styles

This stage demands a significant shift in your parenting approach. There should be no more handholding during this age frame. Strive to transition to a 100% partnership relationship with your high-schooler. Here's how...

- *Clear Boundaries and Expectations*: Make sure that your teenager knows the rules and knows you well as a parent, therefore, they shouldn't be surprised by consequences.
  - I set SOLID boundaries for my child.

- ○ I set expectations for: academics, cleanliness, socializing and household work.

- ○ I hold them accountable.

- *Ownership of Decisions*: My message to them during these years is that they own their decisions, and I am there to assist if needed. The credit of successes and/or failures go to them alone, I emphasize. This fosters independence and responsibility.

- *Intervention as Partnership*: You will, however, intervene if there are noticeable failures on their part, as I do. But the approach remains a partnership: "You will partner with them to correct things or come up with new plans". The key word is partnership. "Allow them the first opportunity to develop their own plan to do things", I advise.

- *Encourage Balance*: I encourage them to involve themselves in something beyond school work to balance their time and thoughts. This could be sports, a part-time job, church, hobbies or exercise.

Reinforcing Core Values: Character, Habits, and True Self

The summer before high school is a crucial time for reinforcing foundational lessons. I dedicated my time to reenforcing lessons on character, study habits and characteristics of good people.

- *Navigating Social Cliques*: I tell them about the typical crowds or cliques that form in high school (jocks, preppy, wanna-be-popular, nerds, bullies, gossipers, druggies, etc.).

- *Authenticity Over Conformity*: Everyone wants to fit-in and feel that they 'belong'...unfortunately, some people will change who they are in the process. I emphasize that "EVERYONE respects those who are true to themselves and honest. I let them know that they don't have to be the best at everything or conform to what the crowd wants...they just need to be REAL and they will be successful. This advice, I believe, is vital for building self-esteem and resilience in a challenging social environment.

Open Lines of Communication: Essential for Guidance

Despite their increasing independence, communication remains paramount. For this age frame, I make it clear that the lines of communication must remain open at all times. They must respond to me when I reach out via phone or text.

When You're Doing It Right, You Will...

Remember that this phase is about evolving your relationship and preparing them for life.

- Transition to Partnership, Not Dictatorship: I loosen the reins. Instead of micromanaging, I try letting them take ownership of their decisions. When they make a mistake, I'm there to say, "I told you so," because *I told you so* is your divine right as a parent. 😌

- I aim to be their guide, not their boss. Let them make mistakes so they can learn from them. Just don't let them do anything that will land them in the back of a police car.

- Teach the ***Art of Hustle***: Guide them without being a drill sergeant.

  - Do NOT figure everything out for them or arrange their "foot-in-the-door". Show them the door and teach them the skills of how to get it opened. If you allow them to leverage everything you have, then where is their <u>grind</u>? their hustle? Do not deprive them of the key skill that helped you succeed. That skill is, "doing whatever you need to do to accomplish your goal"

- "Don't Let the Stupid Win" Rule: Teenagers, sometimes make dumb decisions. My role is to teach them to pause, think, and ask themselves, "Is this stupid?". I help them calculate consequences, like *the distance between the roof and the hospital* if they consider jumping off the roof into a pool.

- Be Their Biggest Cheerleader: I attend their games, performances, or whatever weird niche activity they're into. It matters to them, even if they act like it doesn't. And don't forget to take embarrassing pictures—they'll thank you when they're older. (Or not.).

- Promote Independence: Give teens autonomy while being their safety net. I let them make choices about classes, jobs, and extracurriculars while helping them weigh pros and cons.

- Teach Financial Literacy: I use these years to teach budgeting basics, like balancing a checking account or saving for a car.

- Encourage Goal-Setting: I help them map out short- and long-term goals and show them how to break them into actionable steps.

- Teach Life Skills: Cooking, budgeting, laundry—equip them for independence. If they can't boil an egg by senior year, that's on you.

- **Be Present**: Show up for games, concerts, or even late-night talks about life. They'll remember your presence more than anything else.

- Navigating Social and Academic Pressures Together: High school introduces complex social cliques (jocks, preppy, wanna-be-popular, nerds, bullies, gossipers, druggies, etc.) and intense academic pressures. Fathers in the brotherhood can discuss strategies for teaching authenticity ("be REAL and they will be successful"), encouraging balance with extracurriculars, and guiding future planning for college or careers. Sharing experiences about "Don't Let the Stupid Win" scenarios unifies us dads in teaching practical judgment and resilience in the face of peer pressure and risky decisions.

Survival: Maintaining "open lines of communication" with a teenager can be profoundly challenging, leading to *eye rolls*. Dads can share tips for empathetic listening, creative ways to keep their attention without lecturing, and humor to defuse tension. This mutual support helps us fathers persevere through the "emotional shape-shifters", reinforcing that these experiences are universal and that collective humor and empathy make the teenage rollercoaster more manageable.

- Unified Support for Mothers through Shared Goals: I mentioned this before, but its worth repeating...A father who is actively engaging with his brotherhood about these challenges is better equipped to partner with the mother. By aligning on boundaries, expectations, and future plans, both parents can present a unified front, which is crucial for the teen's stability and growth. This shared commitment inspires mothers by demonstrating a dedicated and collaborative approach to their child's future, reinforcing that they are not alone in guiding their child towards adulthood.

As they move towards graduation and the next phase of their lives, I remind them that closing one door opens another. Keep your finger on the pulse of their life, friends and social groups in high school, college, military or wherever life takes them. This continuous involvement, though adjusted in style, remains essential, demonstrating that being a good father is a long journey that takes the support of other men and fathers, and you are part of that ongoing support. This collective effort empowers us and unifies us in shaping the future generations, making the transition to adulthood smoother and more successful.

CHAPTER 9

Mentor and Consultant: 20 to 25 Years Old

Fostering Independence in Young Adults

Man, I wish parenting ended after the high-school/college-time periods....but it doesn't. This final stage of active parenting requires a delicate, but firm, adjustment of your parental style and focus, shifting into the role of a mentor and consultant, rather than a direct authority. It's a balance of parenting, mentoring and ignoring. My goal is to catapult them into adulthood while they might still try to pull the 'I'm your child" card whenever it's convenient (often when money is involved). This is a crucial time when dads need to ask for help and support from other fathers in navigating the transition of their children into fully independent and self-sufficient adults.

The Delicate Balance: Support vs. Tough Love The biggest challenge in this stage, for me, is knowing when to offer support and when to enforce tough love. The worst thing we can do during this age frame is to coddle/enable them.

- *Adult Expectations*: We MUST treat them like adults and have high expectations of them, I insist. I reiterate that they solely own every decision of their life. You can consult with and offer guidance, but "make it clear to them that the final decision is theirs.

- *Financial Independence*: 4 or 5 years after graduating high school...you no longer 'give' them money; it's now a loan that must be paid back, in some form or fashion (money or sweat). If they pull the "I'm grown" card, but then need money from you, it's time to shift gears. They can't have their cake and eat it too. Gone are the days of handouts—it's now a loan with terms. Have fun charging them interest. This teaches financial responsibility.

- *Budgeting*: I show them how to make a budget, stick to it, and avoid credit card debt. You might humorously note, as I did, that Gen Z thinks they'll retire by becoming TikTok influencers, but serious lessons about saving are vital.

- *Negotiating*: Whether it's a car purchase, job offer, or apartment lease, I show them how to advocate for themselves. I use mock scenarios and ridiculous demands for practice.

> ➤ **Encourage Failure** (the Good Kind) This is the stage where they need to take risks and learn from their mistakes. I resist the urge to swoop in and fix everything.

- *Boundaries for Returning Home*: If they move back in, make sure they know this isn't a five-star hotel. They clean their room, do their laundry, and buy their own groceries. Clear boundaries foster self-sufficiency. Fellas, ask for help from other fathers on how to effectively set boundaries and expectations for young adults.

- *The "Call Your Parents" Rule*: Even as they become fully independent, the connection with me remains vital, I hope. I let them know that no matter how old they get, they still need to call me—preferably more than just when they need something. I use humor: "Hey, remember the guy who wiped your butt for two years? Yeah, he'd love a call every now and then". This reinforces the lifelong nature of your relationship.

- *Mentor Mode*: You're less of a parent and more of a coach. You're there to help them navigate relationships, careers, and the occasional existential crisis.

But remember, the goal isn't to make decisions for them—it's to give them the tools to make their own.

> ➤ **Assess Their Thinking:** As I speak with them, I dip into their lives on occasion to assess how they 'think' about things. I ask about "politics and their position on controversial topics, or their thoughts on budgeting and parenting. This engagement encourages critical thinking and allows you to gauge their maturity.
>
> > o Disclaimer: Remember that your child's age doesn't automatically make them a mature and responsible adult.

- *Healthy Living and Safety*: As they are now living in their own place and beginning their family, I teach them about healthy living, personal safety and family security". Hopefully, they learned most of this from watching you as they were growing up. I remind them that in order to be there to take care of their families, they must first protect themselves and maintain a healthy life. Again, this is much easier for them if they had a dad who demonstrated a healthy and safe life throughout their upbringing (hint, hint).

When You're Doing It Right, You Will...

- <u>Coach, Don't Direct</u>: Your role shifts to that of a mentor.

- <u>Encourage Resilience</u>: Young adults will fail—it's part of growth. I frame failure as a learning opportunity to foster "resilience and perseverance"; a single failure is a data point, not the final destination

- <u>Model Healthy Boundaries</u>: Teach them how to balance work, religion/charity, relationships, and personal time by demonstrating these skills during their teenage years.

- <u>Encourage Independence</u>: Please let them make their own decisions—and their own mistakes. Resist the urge to bail them out every time.

- <u>Foster Growth</u>: Encourage them to take risks, pursue passions, and embrace failure as part of success.

- <u>Be Their Consultant</u>: They'll come to you for advice (money, taxes or cooking). Offer wisdom without judgment.

The Brotherhood in Action: Sustaining Support for Emerging Adults

This final stage of active parenting requires a nuanced balance of support and challenge, and your Diapers and

Dominoes crew is essential for guidance and accountability. This collective commitment empowers us to successfully launch independent adults into the world.

- *Collective Wisdom on "Tough Love" and Financial Boundaries*: Dads in the brotherhood can openly discuss and share strategies for moving from handouts to setting clear financial expectations, and establishing firm boundaries if young adults move back home. This collective wisdom empowers fathers to avoid coddling and ensures a unified, consistent approach to fostering independence, preventing financial strains on both sides.

- *Sharing Life Skills Expertise and Mentorship*: Not every dad is an expert in budgeting, cooking, or negotiating. Collectively, the guys can become a powerful network for sharing practical tips and resources, creating a system where fathers can learn from each other to better equip their young adults. For instance, a father who is an accountant could offer to teach basic tax preparation, while another who is a chef could lead a cooking session for the young adults.

- *Inspiring Mothers with Unified Mentorship*: When fathers are actively engaged in their brotherhood, seeking advice on guiding their young adults through these complex transitions, they demonstrate a profound commitment to their child's well-being. This proactive mentorship **inspires mothers** by showing a dedicated and collaborative approach to their child's future, reinforcing that the parenting journey is a team effort even as children become independent.

The true gift is watching as they respond to the challenge and possibly involve you. This phase of the journey, guided by your wisdom and unwavering support, culminates in their full independence, demonstrating the profound impact of your lifelong commitment as a father. Remember that being a good father is a long journey that takes the support of other men and fathers, for continued growth and perspective.

CHAPTER 10

The Ever-Evolving Dad: A Lifelong Commitment to the Brotherhood

Hopefully, you are at this part because you read the chapters above. If so, THANK YOU. This final chapter brings together the themes of fatherhood as a lifelong commitment, the importance of continuous learning, and the enduring value of a strong male support network. This is the culminating message that, to me, makes this book a must-have, inspiring every man, father, and mother who seeks to understand and cultivate empowered, unified fatherhood.

The Journey Continues: Learning and Growing

I'd be remiss if I did not mention that God has been with me and my family through the years and through all the ups and downs. He has helped me when there were no others around to help or ask You will realize that your child will learn from others, as well as be helped by others who aren't their parents. That's OK. There have been countless times in which something else saved my children from harm and I'm thankful. There have also been occasions in which I had no words to give to heal them from hurt or heartbreak. In those moments, I simply held them. That night or the next day, they were better. A healthy prayer life has always stabilized me when problems came. Believe me... they will come. Whatever your beliefs are, it's important that your kids see your ability to be resilient and handle tough times with your head up.

- <u>Embracing Mistakes</u>: As a dad, you MUST know that you will fail at some things along the way. You will say the wrong stuff, not say enough and miss some important opportunities. The key is to learn from them, get better and don't live off of your previous parenting highlights. Everything you accomplished in the past could easily be overshadowed by one failure. Every day is a fresh start; begin each day with a new commitment and rededication for your child.

- <u>Life's Lessons</u>: As someone wisely said, *"Learning life is different from learning in school...school teaches you the lesson first, then you take the test. Life gives you the test...then you learn the lesson."* That will be true with parenting also. This journey is a continuous test and a continuous learning experience.

- <u>The Secret of Great Parents</u>: **Great parents don't know what the hell they are doing, but they try**

their VERY BEST to do the right thing for their child every day. To them, nothing else is more important. They also realize that the parenting job starts over new each day. This humility and dedication are the hallmarks of true fatherhood.

- The Power of Legacy, Shaping Futures: The impact of your fatherhood stretches far beyond your own lifetime. The bottom line is that it takes a very long time for a person to live up to their fullest potential. The same will be true for your child. You are to ensure that their long road to maturity isn't hindered or delayed as a result of poor parenting.

- Rewarding and Fun: Fatherhood is a tremendous responsibility, but it is also incredibly rewarding and fun as you witness the growth of a life that you helped shape.

- Guiding, Not Duplicating: **The goal is not to make them become like you. Instead, the objective is to instill in them the knowledge and confidence to become anyone they wish and the assertiveness to go for their goals without excuse.** This empowers them to forge their own unique path.

- Shared Imperfection: As they navigate their own lives and perhaps become parents themselves, remind them that they are not perfect, because you were not perfect. Share the humorous story again:

Remind them that you are the same guy who put the baby's booty thermometer in your mouth....but you survived that mistake and many more. They will survive also. This reminds them of humility, resilience, and the power of learning from mistakes.

A Call to Ongoing Brotherhood and Unified Support

The "Diapers and Dominoes" concept, and indeed this entire book, began with my premise that men need to support, encourage and reprimand each other. This need does not diminish as your children grow; it evolves. Your personal brotherhood, established through events like the guys-only baby shower, becomes a lifelong resource for shared wisdom, accountability, and emotional support. The journey of fatherhood is long, complex, and deeply personal, yet it is profoundly enriched by the collective experience of other men. This book inspires confidence, fosters collaboration, and strengthens the entire family unit by emphasizing the crucial role of an engaged, supported father.

Thank you for embarking on this fatherhood revolution with me. May your journey be filled with love, laughter, growth, healthy children and the unwavering, unified support of your brotherhood.

THANK YOU to all the fathers that I've learned from throughout my life. There are many other coworkers, acquaintances and even strangers that I've learned from. I wanted you all to know that I've either learned something valuable from you and/or became a better father because of you.

Dennis Cail Sr*   John Perry*   Lance White
         Herman Chambers*   Dennis Cail Jr
Anthony Carey   Bernard Hammonds
    John Varner Sr*   Dontrell Cail   John Varner Jr
Quintin Robinson Sr   Darryl Jones
     Jason Wade   John Hearld   Darren Talley
Dennis Cail III   Karl Northrop   Michael Anderson
             Tony Ross   Quintin Robinson Jr
Jeremiah Waldon   Thomas Mack   Elgin McDowell
     Harold Wright   Sway Cannon
Kendall Thomas   Shawn Marion   Duke Pettijohn
         Tim Carpenter   Thomas Perry*
Melvin Allen*   Leroy Allen*   Corey McCrary
     Chris Perry   Bobby Lloyd   Ali Yusef
         Todd Hamilton   John Bennett
         Ryan Berg   Kevin Thomas

APPENDIX

Guys-Only Baby Showers

There are several baby shower themes that will suit the dad and his guest well. The goal is to consider the dad and the guest list, then select the theme that will provide the most fun for the collection of guys. I have been doing these for years and I honestly do not have a favorite theme...the amount of fun will depend on the group of guys. We use the term Diapers and Dominoes loosely because it's the theme that started it all ☺. For example, a friend of mine called me up one day and said, "Hey Cail!, I want you to host a Diapers and Dominoes party for me". In reality, however, he had a Pampers and Poker theme. It has become acceptable to refer to a guys-only baby shower as *Diapers and Dominoes*. With that said, please review the summary of each theme below; it will give you the foundation to begin planning a great time.

I. Diapers and Dominoes

A. Overview...

- *Location:* house or apartment or clubhouse or lounge

- *Recommended number of guys:* unlimited

- *Main supplies:* diapers (any brand), dominoes, pen/paper (for scoring), bib for dad (and 2 safety pins to pin it to his shirt), music, drinks and appetizers, TV and camera/video

- *Most important piece:* someone to plan everything and make sure all supplies are ready

- *Setup and decorations:* We're guys...so no decorations, but setup is important...set the table with: baby food jars, baby bottles, dominoes and large bib for dad; Dad must bring or wear a white T-shirt for guest to sign

- *Primary activities:* playing dominoes, drinking from baby bottles, taking shots from baby food jars, music, conversations around the table

- *Gifts:* No gifts, however, if someone wants to give a gift...he can buy a gift card (Amazon, Walmart, Visa Gift Card, Home Improvement) or from a baby store

B. Details...

Prior to the party...If the host thinks ALL the guys will consume a lot of alcohol, he should advise everyone to leverage their Ride-Share service or plan to sleep-over.

The guy(s) who planned this, need to show up 30 to 45 minutes early to set up everything. This includes:

- ✓ re-arranging furniture,
- ✓ setting up chairs,
- ✓ organizing the domino table,
- ✓ turning on the music and/or TV,
- ✓ ordering/cooking food if necessary,
- ✓ placing the drinks on ice or in refrigerator and
- ✓ washing out the baby food jars (AKA 'shot glasses').

Yes, you read that correctly; the guys will take shots of their favorite drink from clean Gerber food jars. That has always been one of the coolest features of D.A.D. The dad MUST eat one jar of fruit baby food (banana or apple sauce) and one vegetable baby food. Buy enough baby food jars so that there is enough for everyone to have a shot glass and there are 2 extra UNOPENED jars for the games. Guests are not required to eat the baby food; they are permitted to dump it out and clean their jar.

Please take A LOT of pictures and record as much video as possible! It is so great to watch these later; you will likely laugh harder while watching it on video. We also would love to see these on the "Diapers and Dominoes" Facebook page), so all fathers can share in the fun 😊

Additionally, all guys will drink their beverage of choice from large baby bottles. The terms "Poppin Bottles" and "Bottle Service" will take on a whole new meaning for guys-only baby showers (LOL 😊) When the dad-to-be arrives, he is required to sterilize his baby bottle and the bottle's nipple by boiling them for 5 minutes. Following that, he must cut a slightly larger hole in the nipple (allows you to drink faster).

The next task for the dad is to prepare his white T-shirt so guests can sign it. With a permanent black marker, the dad will write the following:

Write on Front: (D.A.D.) Who's Got my Back Back? On the back write: I Got Your Back!

As the guests arrive, instruct them to:

(1) place their purchased diapers and gift cards in an designated area,

(2) if they brought food, tell them where to place the food

(3) grab a baby bottle and prepare themselves a drink

(4) Write their name on the back of dad's T-shirt

(5) Give the host their keys if they plan on drinking alcohol (no exceptions)

Once everyone arrives, have someone say a short prayer for the baby and the parents... then begin the fun. You will have the most fun around the game table as you talk, tell jokes about the dad and just be silly. See the "Ideas" chapter for suggestions on things to do during the party. Customize it to your liking. The party should not last more than 3 hours.

If you do a good job of returning home at a reasonable hour, it's possible that your girlfriend or wife would not mind you having a monthly guys-night-out That's just a thought ☺ and it has worked for others in the past. I've seen the opposite happen as well...LMAO...the dad-to-be shows up 6 hours later and drunk, then the mom goes ballistic. She yells, punches him, questions his ability to be a father and locks him out... You catch my drift ☺

One of the hidden benefits to D.A.D. is the pictures and videos of the party that will be shared with the expecting mom and others. The pictures always come out great and capture CRAZY moments. All-in-all, it makes those who were not there very jealous, because you had an amazing time. At the end of the night, EVERYONE must help clean-up. Each guy must take his Gerber shot glass and baby bottle home as a souvenir (and as evidence that he was actually at a baby shower). The dad must also gather all the diapers to take home with him.

The host is responsible for monitoring everyone's alcohol intake. Please have water available throughout the evening and check everyone before they leave. Don't return keys to those who had too much to drink...allow them to sober up, ride-share or stay overnight. (Please forgive me if I sound a bit "preachy"...but drunk driving is a REAL threat to your life and others on the road. It doesn't make sense to risk ending a life after celebrating a new life). As a part of the initial planning and invites, let the potential guests know that they should ride-share (Lyft / Uber) if they plan to drink anything.

II. Pampers and Poker

A. Overview...this is very similar to the Diapers and Dominoes option above; I copied/pasted a lot of the same info. Poker night is the difference.

- *Location:* house or apartment or clubhouse
- *Recommended number of guys:* unlimited
- *Key supplies:* diapers (Pampers brand), deck of cards, poker chips, bib for dad (and 2 safety pins to pin it to his shirt), music, drinks and appetizers, TV
- *Most important piece:* someone to facilitate everything (coordinate the activities)

- *Setup and decorations:* We're guys...so, No decorations! Setup is important, however...set the table with: baby food jars, baby bottles, deck of cards and poker chips; Dad must bring or wear a white T-shirt
  - o *If you are playing poker for money, let all guys know the minimum amount to bring to purchase poker chips.* Each poker hand can be as low as $1, $5, $10, etc. The goal is to make it friendly. The winner splits half the 'profit' with the dad-to-be; if the dad wins, then he should share some of the profit with the host/facilitator.
- *Primary activities:* playing poker, drinking alcohol from baby bottles, taking shots from baby food jars, conversations around the table
- *Gifts:* No gifts, however, if someone wants to give a gift...he can buy a gift card (Amazon, Walmart, Visa Gift Card, Home Improvement) or from a baby store

B. Details...

Prior to the party...If the host thinks ALL the guys will consume a lot of alcohol, he should make arrangements for shared rides. As a part of the initial planning and invites, let the potential guests know that they should take a Lyft or an Uber if they plan to drink anything.

The guy(s) who planned this, need to show up 30 to 45 minutes early to set up everything. This includes: re-arranging furniture, setting up chairs, organizing the poker table, dividing the poker chips ($200 for each player), turning on the music and/or TV, ordering/cooking food if necessary, placing the drinks in ice or refrigerator and washing out the baby food jars (AKA 'shot glasses'). Yes, you read that correctly; the guys will take shots of their favorite drink from clean baby food jars. The dad MUST eat one jar of fruit baby food (banana or apple sauce) and one vegetable baby food. That has always been one of the coolest features of D.A.D. Buy enough baby food jars so that there is enough for everyone to have a shot glass and there are 2 extra UNOPENED jars for the games.

All guys will drink their beverage of choice from large baby bottles. When the dad-to-be arrives, he is required to sterilize his baby bottle and the bottle's nipple by boiling them for 5 minutes. Following that, he must cut a slightly larger hole in the nipple...this allows more fluid to pass through the nipple faster. The next task for the dad is to prepare his white T-shirt so guests can sign it. With a permanent black marker, the dad will write the following:

Write on Front: (D.A.D.) Who's Got my Back Back? On the back write: I Got Your Back!

As the guests arrive, instruct them to:

a. place their purchased diapers and gift cards in an designated area,

b. if they brought food, tell them where to place the food

c. grab a baby bottle and prepare themselves a drink

d. Write their name on the back of dad's T-shirt

e. Give the host their keys if they plan on drinking alcohol (no exceptions)

Once everyone arrives, have someone say a short prayer for the baby, dad and mom, then begin the fun. Explain the rules for the poker game that you will play. Most parties I've been to have selected Texas Hold'em style games. It's easy to learn for the 1st-time player. It's runs a lot smoother when there is a skilled dealer. You will have the most fun around the game table as you talk, tell jokes about the dad and just be silly. See the "Ideas" chapter for suggestions on things to do during the party. Customize it to your liking; the goal is to ensure that all guests are involved. The party should not last more than 3.5 hours.

Again, one of the hidden benefits to D.A.D. is the pictures and videos of the party that will be shared with the expecting mom and others. The pictures always come out great and capture CRAZY moments. All-in-all, it makes those who were not there very jealous, because you had an amazing time. Please submit these to our Diapers and Dominoes social media group, so the world can see 😊

The host is responsible for monitoring everyone's alcohol intake. Please have water available throughout the evening and check everyone before they leave. Don't return keys to those who had too much to drink...allow them to sober up or stay overnight. (Again, I do not mean to be "preachy"...but please do not let buzzed or drunk driving define your evening and ruin it)

III. Luvs and Laughs

A. Overview...

- *Location:* Comedy Club
- *Recommended number of guys:* at least 4
- *Key supplies:* Luvs brand diapers, Money - for entry, appetizers and drinks; Dad must wear a baby sling, with toy baby in it (picture Allen, from the old Hangover movie, in the elevator ☺) Dad must wear white T-shirt or bring the shirt along (if venue has a strict dress code) and a black permanent marker
- *Most important piece:* someone to plan and coordinate – buy tickets or make reservations, send invites and text messages to attendees

- *Setup:* get the comedy host and/or comedians involved IN ADVANCE to joke on dad and the challenges of fatherhood.

- *Primary activities:* Enjoying the show, hanging out with the boys, drinking and playing games (see "Ideas" chapter)

- *Gifts:* If someone wants to give a gift...buy a gift card from a super store (Walmart, Target, baby store or Amazon)

B. Details...

This is also a very cool event to have. To set things in motion, identify the comedy clubs in the area. View their websites to determine the schedule of shows and comedian line-up. Of course, if the dad has a favorite comedian coming to town prior to the baby's arrival, plan to go to that show. ☺ If you are unfamiliar with a comedian, you can look on the internet to watch previous shows they've performed in.

Once you've selected a date for the event, find out how to get tickets. Buy tickets early if there is assigned seating. The goal is to sit in the front, close to the stage. If the tickets are general admission, then plan on arriving very early, so everyone can sit near the front. This is because we want the comedians and MC to see and engage the dad and his friends.

If everyone will drink, plan on taking a shared ride. If someone, who's responsible, wants to volunteer to be the designated driver then he can drive everyone to/from the comedy venue.

Call the comedy club to find out how they handle special requests for things like birthdays, anniversaries and uhhhhhh.....baby showers. You are basically inquiring about what must be done to involve the MC and comedians in the Luvs and Laughs celebration. When you arrive at the comedy club, introduce yourself to the host/manager/MC and let them know what you are celebrating.

At the end of the night, get as many people as possible to sign dad's white T-shirt and be sure to take pictures with the comedians. You will have the most fun around the table throughout the show, especially when the comedians are involved. See the "Ideas" chapter for suggestions on things to do during the party. Customize it to your liking. The event should not last more than 4 hours.

IV. Huggies and Happy Hour

A. Overview...

- *Location:* Sports Bar or Restaurant
- *Recommended number of guys:* up to 10
- *Key supplies:* Huggies brand diapers, money for appetizers and drinks, Dad must wear a baby sling, with toy baby in it. Dad must wear white T-shirt or bring the shirt along (if venue has a strict dress code) and a black permanent marker
- *Most important piece:* someone to plan and coordinate –make reservations (if the place is typically crowded), send RSVP invites
- *Setup and decorations:* Ask hostess to seat you in the center of the restaurant (no booth) or if it's open seating.....simply fine a table where dad can be seen by most people; ask the staff to bring a high-chair and a kids menu/crayons/balloon for dad
- *Primary activities:* talking around the table, joking, drinking and playing games (see "Ideas" chapter)
- *Gifts:* If someone wants to give a gift...buy a gift card from a super store or a Visa gift card

B. Details...

This is probably the simplest baby shower to arrange. I've seen this option used at the last minute or when the planner doesn't have a lot of time to organize any of the other options.

For Huggies and Happy Hour all you need is a place/time to meet and the key supplies mentioned above. The more wait-staff you involve in your party, the more fun you will have. Give them permission to join in on the fun and pull gags on dad. Choose a bar/restaurant that's known to be lively and fun. Preferably, select a place with tall tables, TVs with sports on, music and nice-looking people. Try to sit in a location in the center of the restaurant/bar...don't hide in a corner. By doing this, more people will come by and wish the dad well.

The dad can either wear the plain white T-shirt or bring it with him for others to sign. Take lots of pictures and be careful not to overspend. Look for drink/food specials and set spending limits for yourself. You should not walk out of the place thinking, "WOW! I spent far more money than I wanted to!" That's a sucky feeling. The dad does not pay for his food; he is free to leave a gratuity, but he is not responsible for the bill.

At the end of the night, get as many people as possible to sign dad's white T-shirt and be sure to take pictures with the staff and strangers. You will have the most fun around the table and involving restaurant staff. Again, see the "Ideas" chapter for suggestions on things to do during the party. Customize it to your liking. This event should not last more than 3 hours.

Planning

DON'T do a half-ass job planning...do it right

<u>*30 + days before event*</u>

- Choose one of the 4 themes one month in advance
- The Planner should be familiar enough with the dad-to-be to determine which theme he'd like. If not, it is OK to allow the dad-to-be to choose.
- If you plan to do Diapers and Dominoes or Pampers and Poker...Pick a date **at least 30 days** prior to the event...to do it right, it requires at least this much time. Begin at least 21 days in advance if you are planning Huggies and Happy Hour or Luvs and Laughs.
- Someone needs to be the Planner and someone needs to ensure that the messages go out to everyone who will attend. This person could be the dad-to-be, however, if at all possible...let someone else do it. After all, the dad-to-be is the guest of honor.

29 to 25 days before event

- Choose location and time of the event
- Gather a guest list from dad-to-be and other close friends. Specifically, get everyone's mobile number.

24 to 20 days before event

- For Huggies and Happy Hour or Luvs and Laughs, planning begins here
- No matter which event theme you choose, at 3 weeks before the event....Send everyone a text message about the event. Include the occasion, theme, date and time. Tell everyone to reply to you with their e-mail address because you will send them the details of how to prepare for the event.

19 to 15 days before event

- Get confirmation from everyone who plans to attend by sending an Evite.com invitation to their e-mail or mobile device. Include a contact phone # in the invitation.
- Look at the Shopping List for the selected theme. Decide whether one or two people will buy everything (others will repay them) or if the list will be divided evenly. *The goal is to "share the financial load" so no one will spend too much money.*

- Start gathering money from attendees if everyone will pitch in for supplies or split the load and text each person telling them what to bring (this only works if you have dependable friends). *I suggest that the planner/host purchase all the critical items for the event and have others reimburse him via Zelle or CashApp or other payment apps.*

- Confirm the event's location (house, apartment (clubhouse), sports bar, comedy club, etc. *Make sure the venue KNOWS that you are coming on a specific date...reserve it.*

14 to 10 days before event

- Text and email attendees reminding them of what to bring

- If money is required the day of the event, tell everyone how much to bring

- Decide who will take pictures and video during the event. Get a relative, friend or one of the attendees to assume this duty. The purpose for this is to capture the event, share it with the mother-to-be, family and social networks ("**Diapers and Dominoes**" Facebook page) *This is the fun part and the memories will last forever.*

- Begin purchasing items

9 to 5 days before event

- Ask everyone to verify that they have purchased their diapers and other requested items
- If money is required the day of the event, remind everyone of how much to bring
- Call the venue to confirm reservations and verify that everything is going according to plan.

4 to 2 days before event

- Gather all important items for Diapers and Dominoes or Pampers and Poker
- For Luvs and Laughs, contact comedy club to determine who to speak to on the night of the event (Manager's name? Host's name?). Basically, you want them to support your party and have them ask the comedians to add a joke or 2 about the dad-to-be/fatherhood
- Assign designated driver(s) or arrange for safe transportation for those who might go over the legal alcohol limit for driving. ***Please take my advice on this! Nothing ruins a great night like a DWI/DUI or even worse...critical injuries or death.***

1 day before event

- Let everyone know that everything is ready and you're looking forward to having a great time tomorrow. Send time and address location in text message and e-mail.

Event Day

- Show up on time!
- Have Fun!
- DO NOT allow the dad-to-be to get drunk. <u>This is not a bachelor party</u>, it's a party to celebrate the coming of a new child. Yes, the dad can drink alcohol if he wishes...however, the goal is to ensure he has fun, he remembers everything and he's able to get home without incident.

Ideas and Activities to Consider

- Order alcohol that comes in blue containers if u know it's a boy
- Call and have the radio station give a shout out to the dad-to-be
- Have non-alcoholic drinks and water on hand for those who don't drink alcohol
- Use baby food jars for shots
- Use large plastic baby bottles for beer and cocktails
- Post pictures on social media sites
- Assign designated drivers in advance and plan Lyft/ Uber rides

- Have dad sterilize bottle tops
- Suggested menu: wings, mini sandwiches, chips, dip, nuts, crackers, fruit
- Have a sports game on or a classic dad/kid type movie (i.e. Daddy Daycare, 3 Men and a Baby, etc)
- When everyone arrives, pray for the baby and the family, friends and others that will care for the baby
- Take lots of pictures (1 person or everyone uses phone cameras)
- Anyone that talks or texts on their phone to a female must immediately donate $5 to the Host
- Hire 1 or 2 people to make and serve drinks
- Take a shot each time a baby is shown on TV
- Conversations around the table: (a) Funny dad stories, (b)challenges of raising a boy or a girl, (c)How women make it hard to be a dad, (d) what Not to do as a dad (lessons learned); (e) previous girlfriends who would be terrible mothers; (f) who do you know that's a good dad or appears to be a good dad; (g) what features do you want the baby to have from you and which features from the mother (h) What's the difference in raising a child today compared to 20 years ago

- Video tape each attendee separately... sending the father-to-be well wishes and giving advice. Send dad/mom video via text
- Have dad wear backpack with doll in it and wear bib (w/pacifier) during event
- Dad gets a tattoo 30 days after birth: baby shoe with baby's birth date

Games

- Alphabet name game, select letter, go in circle providing a baby name, you take a shot if you can't think of a name in 3 seconds
- Dad dress baby(doll) for the winter and place in car seat (Host to get with baby's mom in advance for the supplies)
- Change diapers race...winner gets a prize (buy 2 toy babies) The winner is the guy who finishes first, without 'hurting'/roughing up the doll ⍰
- Select best name for baby (text the winning girl name and winning boy name to mother-to-be)
- Get the diaper bag and baby ready in 5 minutes (hide items for dad to find)
- Beer chugging race with baby bottles
- In a circle, each attendee says a toast to the dad one at a time; video record

- Guess and write down length and weight of baby; write in sticky notes or index cards. Include your name on the card and make sure that the dad-to-be takes them home
- Set timers/reminders for the dad-to-be to perform various duties throughout the event (change diaper, feed baby, bathe baby, burp baby, pacify/nurture baby)

Shopping List

Diapers and Dominoes or Pampers and Poker

-Sandwiches

-Wings

-Chips

-Salsa

-Nuts and mints

-Fruit/vegetable tray

-Bottled water

-Soda and drink mixers

-Beer (BYOB or get everyone's favorite)

-Alcohol (BYOB or get a list)

-Paper plates

-Cups

-Forks/Spoons/Napkins

- -Small Gerber food jars
- -Baby bottles
- -Diapers
- -Gift card
- -Prizes
- -Dominoes/Cards/Poker Chips
- -Permanent black marker, pen and paper

Huggies and Happy Hour or Luvs and Laughs

- -Small box of Huggies/Luvs
- -Baby Carrier and Pacifier w/clip
- -money for appetizers
- -money for drinks
- -Permanent black marker
- -large baby bottles
- -Gift card

DIAPERS AND DOMINOES (D.A.D.)